APPLAUSE

Carol Muske

Applause

University of Pittsburgh Press

Published by the University of Pittsburgh Press, Pittsburgh, Pa. 15260
Copyright © 1989, Carol Muske
All rights reserved
Feffer and Simons, Inc., London
Manufactured in the United States of America

Library of Congress Cataloging in Publication Data

Muske, Carol, 1945–
  Applause / Carol Muske.
    p. cm. — (Pitt poetry series)
    ISBN 0-8229-3613-5.   ISBN 0-8229-5417-6 (pbk.)
  I. Title. II. Series.
PS3563.U837A87   1989
811'.54—dc19   88-29086
                                       CIP

The author and publisher wish to express their grateful acknowledgment to the following publications in which some of these poems first appeared: *American Poetry Review* ("After Care," "Box," and "Dream"); *Antioch Review* ("Monk's House, Rodmell"); *Field* ("Vermont Farmhouse"); *Missouri Review* ("Immunity"); *The New Yorker* ("Skid" and "Summer Cold"); *Southern California Anthology* ("Asbestos"); *Threepenny Review* ("Pediatrics"); *Verse* ("Ideal"); and *Western Humanities Review* ("The Wish Foundation").

"Box" was awarded a Pushcart Press Prize for 1987–88. "Summer Cold" was also published in *New York/Beijing,* an American-Chinese anthology, 1987, and *Writing Our Lives,* a British-American anthology of women's poetry, 1988, Camden Press. "Asbestos" and "Applause" were published in the *Poets Respond to AIDS* anthology, 1989.

Thanks to the National Endowment for the Arts and the Ingram Merrill Foundation.

The publication of this book is supported by grants from the National Endowment for the Arts in Washington, D.C., a Federal agency, and the Pennsylvania Council on the Arts.

For Annie Cameron
and Kelsey

Contents

APPLAUSE

Dream

It's my old apartment, Gramercy Park,
but then it's not. I know the three steps up,
the squeaking door, the foyer table
stacked with mail, I know the light falling
like jail bars on the tiles, my numbered door.
But when I turn the key, there's a disco,
strobes, my dead landlord serving drinks.
Or it's a skating rink, a nook at the Frick.
Today I woke from sorting something in my head—
a box of old mittens or scarves,
snowflake patterns, shooting stars.
Here I have a poster on my wall:
the sun in shades, a turtleneck of smog.
It isn't just a dropped stitch,
my memory's actively unfurnishing that flat—
why, I haven't a clue. But one, perhaps.
The time I stood, locked out,
on the snowy fire escape, looking through
the glass at my life: lamps, books.
coffee table, each self-contained photograph.
New York at dawn, my flame silk dress
feel improvised now—it was that interior
I'd fix in my sight forever,
climb down the icy rungs and not come back.
Freezing wind out there, stocking feet,
my dress filling like a bell—
then a newer, dizzying grip on things,
this sudden hungry wish for riddance,
to turn my back on space I'd made,
with the pathetic charm of the possessive,
mine and uninhabitable.

Summer Cold

By day, she's not so sick. She hits
the hound, then kisses him: nice dog.
He cringes, then his wolfish face lights up.
To me, she does the same. At two, her love
of power's in two parts: love and power.
Late at night, I hold her to my breast—
the wet indent her fevered head makes
stays pressed against my gown. She doesn't
have to ask, I wake with her. I hold
the mercury up to the light and read
its red suspense, the little trapped horizon
of her heat. Her slowed lungs draw
and empty. Below, on the lawn,
a hunched figure—dawn?—rakes the black
grass light, turns into a set of swings,
I hold her sleeping weight and rock
till something in the east throbs up.
Day, offering itself, then drawing back.
Day, commuting from a city remote as hell,
or health, where I remember living once,
for myself. Long before this little bird
filled its throat outside the beveled glass,
before the headlines stumbled on the step.

The Wish Foundation

O holy talk show host,
who daily gives us twenty minutes,
no holds barred, on loneliness,

who has provided, for my particular
amusement, this fat hairy man
in a T-shirt that says he likes sex,

pronouncing himself an "impressionistic
person": describe now for us the child
sent by the Wish Foundation. Hold up

her photograph, say haltingly, that
she died and is buried here,
as per her last request: to fly to

Los Angeles. Then to fly forever beneath
its shocked geologic expression.
To land in Los Angeles, like Persephone

descending the sunset stairs, out of a sky
the color of pomegranate, and through the curved glass
of the ambulance hatch—to be photographed through

the lengthening reflections of exit signs. Persephone
crossing eight lanes, in the rapids of pure oxygen,
descending, recasting the tidy shape of elegy.

Under the overpass, where kids throw
things down on cars, through the gates
and over the machined hills to machined

stones: descending to be where she wished to be.
Where on clear days you can see the city.
Where you can see down the coast

to the cones of the reactor, settling
on the slide, down to the famous rides
of the famous amusement park

where they load the kids into bolted seats
and spin them around a center fixed, but
on a moving foundation. O talk show host,

somebody had to imagine it: how
they would slide hard into what happens.
Fear and desire for more fear. No despair,

would you say? but that sense of black acceleration,
like a blacker wish. I'd say Grief put that new
dress on her. Grief combed her adorable hair.

Then: *which hand* said friendly old Death.
And she stepped away from the foundation
into a sky that all my life, dear

host, I've seen fill and refill
with indifferent valediction: overhead
those stupid planes from the base

flying wing to wing and their shadows
on the earth, somebody's stupid
idea of perfect symmetry.

Skid

Where the snow effigies stood
hard-packed and hosed to ice
in front of the frat houses,
in the middle of the little bridge
over the stopped river,
my leased car spun three times

before the chainless tires caught.
Each time round I saw a face:
the man who imagined he loved me,
the woman who confided in me,
the child who cried "no" upon meeting me,
as if he saw at once to what use

we put those vanishing invented selves.
The slurred tracks, ringed dark
on the outbound path, froze and unfroze
for weeks after the party to celebrate spring.
Down the road, the local museum
considered the Ice Age. The glacier

slid in and out of its lit shape
through a fan of color transparencies,
each ray labelled with an age, a thaw,
the gauged bed of the moraine. Showed how
the ice junkheap hauled the broken shapes
in which we live, cave and gully and flat.

And a further dissolution, part of
a shape we would not recognize for centuries,—
like the coins that tumble down the dark slide
to the weighted spar that triggers the mechanism
that lifts the needle to the jukebox disk: "Blue Moon"—
you saw it standing like an atomic field,

charged with particles: little "you"s and "me"s,
estranged suddenly from the vanity of their motion—
and the prefigured feel of it, music and moon,
turning full force into its mindless will
then stopping, my foot on the accelerator.

Box

Where her right index fingernail should be—
there is a razorblade—
and the black-haired inmate pushes
the smaller one to the wall.

I remember it happening as I came
down the hall, with my copy
of the *The Voice That Is Great Within Us:*

the two figures, one hunched over
the other, the blade hand hovering,
ablaze, then moving across and down.

Today, in the window,
a crystal spins on a bit
of fishline, throwing off light

like netted koi, shiny ruptures
on the ceiling. My small daughter climbs up
its trembling ladder,

extends her small beautiful hand.
In the perfect center of the glass
there is resistance to the image: a room

too brightly lit, in the basement
of the old House of Detention,
where I taught the dazzling inconsistencies—

Pictures in the Mind—
under the Watch Commander's
electric map: its red neon eye-slits

blinking each time a door cracked
within the walls. The women
gravely scrawling on Rainbow

tablets: not graffiti, but poems wrenched
from the same desire to own something—
to tie the tourniquet of style,

the mind's three or four known
happy endings clamped tight
on the blood jet. Love poems to a pimp,

for example: she would never say
he beat her. No, he held her close,
he was "capable of love"—

he was like the elegy
written for the little one
whose mother tried to make her fly:

he would stay suspended in the air.
No one would see that child
screaming, step by step, along the gritty ledge.

If she'd lived, she might have become
the one who thought she wrote songs
like Billie Holiday, or the one

who plagiarized peacefully, week after week,
the poems of Langston Hughes.
Nobody writes anything that moves

across and down the face
of mortal anguish. That cutting tool
found in no book nor

in the exquisite, denatured vision
of invention—page after page
of Pictures in the Mind—but

I taught it right after all.
There were images for her,
                              this mother,

taking back the face she made—
with her bright, revisionist blade—
too ugly, too fat, too stupid
to be loved

and an image for that sudden spidery blood
on the tiles, somewhere the red eye
tracking my impulse
as I pushed open the warning door,

then stood back, catching
the baby at the window—
her open hands, the moving light

she holds at the source
but cannot still.

The Eulogy

The man in the black suit delivers a eulogy
each page he turns, turns
a page of light on the ceiling,

because death mimics us, mocking
the eye's cowardly flight
from the flower-covered coffin

to the framed photo of the bereaved, alive.
It is not night.
It is California.

There are hibiscus dropping
their veined shrouds
on the crushed-stone path outside.

A gold cuff link blazes
as the eulogist raises his hands.

Shadows alter the ceiling,
the readable text.
There are two ways to meet death,

he says. One fearful,
the other courageous.
One day purposeful, the next hopeless,

A young man died because he had sex.
The eulogist speaks of soldiers under fire,
the cowards and the heroes.

The woman next to me cannot stop
weeping. I can find no tears inside
me. The cuff links beam

signals at us, above us.
The sun through the skylight
grows brighter and brighter:

Watch now, God,
Watch the eulogist raise his hands.
The rays, like your lasers,

blind the front rows.
The gifts love gives us!
Some of us flinch, some do not.

Ideal

Though my little daughter owns an Ideal farmyard
let me not direct her attention to
the bloody auction block, the rented backhoe
reversing the plow on the earth,
the iron of the farmer's hand dropped on nothingness.

I know that pain has its tradition,
the slaughtering blade,
the black blood pounded into the grain.
The dreaming animals that come to drink

at this trough understand no tradition,
but I can make the cattle speak
as mildly as they have ever spoken,
the night moths appear as harmless messengers.

The woman who is standing over there
under the tree near the fenceposts,
touching the carved initials—

she is harder to invent.
In a fairy tale, she would be the familiar,
privileged trespasser: she might even be what she is,
a former owner on disputed land.

See her eyes repossess the well,
the porch, the propped-up Ford?
A man in love with speed used to drive it,

its tailpipe a red comet
down the lonely roads. My daughter
wants to know who she is, how does she fit
in the picture, the green painted pasture?

Everyone thinks they can make her put down
the rags and the can of kerosene,
maybe the dear little local paper

14

will crown her queen of the burning trees,
the dynamited dam. It's written in
her two-word tattoo what she will do
and it's written to you

on such a bright night, moon on the fenceposts,
the cow lowing softly, the ideal sky
split open suddenly with stars.

Ex-Embassy

*Sometimes, at dawn, I think I hear
the high sobbing cry of the muezzin
hanging in the sky before it's light
but then, I drop off to sleep again.*

Behind us is the ex-embassy.
Its pool a blue mosaic through
our hedge. The old man
in robe and wrapped head no longer

comes to mop the tiled edge—
his whole morning's work
fragmented by our wall of leaves.
No arm in a rolled sleeve,

bending, lifting. No flashing sections
of aluminum pole fit into a blue mesh scoop
for whisking up floating petals.
No close up: like a Cubist inset,

a turbanned man sipping tea,
eyebrow and striped cup,
slice of a woman's profile
black half-veil, two eyes

yoked in khol moving in a hand-held
mirror. No sun machine-gunning
that round of glass. No part
of a lamb turning on part of a spit.

No peacock opening a bit
of its promiscuous fan.
No cook hurrying the meat
with jagged curses. No meat.
No god. No medallion front,
officially defaced,

16

                    the cornices deflagged
as bare, crude evidence
of our power to invade,
theirs to resist.

A For Sale sign likens it
to a house on a cloud,
a sunrise mosque. It has
patterned tiles with sickles

of wheat or hashish. And wickets,
a *porte cochère* engemmed
with rotating spots.
Maybe a neighbor, through

a closing door,
saw grown men cry out
in a frenzy, on a cold floor,
to a god no one comprehends.

No one comprehends how,
like the god of the broken, rusted lamp,
once out, uncramped,
                    he's *not*.

Not anything you could imagine
not any servant
but the familiar reductive infinite—
lines of fuel drums, phone wires.
Rolled up in the bottom of a child's red valise,

timing devices, threads of plastique . . .
left behind for the doubters,
the personal grit of some other deity,
some intoxicating tattooed Allah

above the human ruins, head in hand.
Not that. Not this. In the garden,
a broken rope of amber beads,
within each separate bead
the lights of patrols go by,
elongate—the next night and the next—

> *what I don't know*
> *but learn to dread*
> *turns over slowly in my bed.*

Intensive Care

—for Kathy and Jim

Then, at 3 A.M., I see her bend
over the stricken infant, her face
that face reproduced for us so many times

in art, as a historical moral:
whose love endureth even death,
whose beauty is forebearance.

Her face that mask of serenity
I see now derives simply
from a shattered will.

There is nothing left of pain or panic—
The TV on the wall tuned to a sitcom.
Her faith in life folded once, twice,

then passed, like a flag
over a lowering coffin,
into her waiting hands.

Far back in its unthinking regions
the brain latches its black shutters
against such improving light

as reason or resignation—the angel
beckoning at the burning gate.
She sees no reason not to draw up

the eyelids, to find herself
reflected in new immensity—
not mother but madonna,

not this child but that other child,
thriving again and returned here
for her to hold and sing to.

Perfectly formed in her arms,
blessed and saved, till the attendants
notice her powerful blind gaze,

till the machines start their desperate,
high-pitched complaints.

Pediatrics

When she came to visit me, I turned my face to the wall—
though only that morning, I'd bent my head at the bell
and with the host on my tongue, mumbled thanks.

Cranked up, then down in my bed—
I told the nurses jokes,
newly precocious, but too old

at twelve, to be anything
but a patient. I slouched in my robe
among the other child-guests of St. Joseph,

the parrot-eyed scald masks,
the waterheads and harelips,
the fat girl with the plastic shunt.

The old crippled nun on her wheeled
platform dispensed her half-witted blessings,
then was gone like the occasional covered gurneys

sliding by my numbered door. Gone
told me I'd go away too—
orderly as dusk in the brick courtyard:

the blank windows curtained one by one.
I could not abide that yearning face
calling me home. Like the Gauls,

in my penciled translations: I saw
Caesar was my home. Through the streets
of the occupied city, his gold mask rose, implacable.

In the fervent improvisational style of the collaborator—

I imagined pain not as pain
but the flickering light embedded
in the headboard, the end

of the snake-wire uncoiling from
the nurses' station. The painkiller winked
in its paper cup, its bleak chirp

meant respect should be paid
for the way I too wielded oblivion,
staring at the wall till six,
my gifts unopened in her lap,

the early dark deepening between us.

Vermont Farmhouse, 3 A.M.

All week she'd felt another's presence
in the house, somebody beseeching but proud,
something dissatisfied. Rounding a corner,
she caught its dark shape drifting in the glass
and under the cellar stairs felt it brood
among the pinnacles and jars, the pickles
and blossom honey. Pushing the pump handle
down, her hand shot back; the first sound
from that rusted mouth—an infant's ravaged cry.
She left the pitcher rolling and stood
at the foot of the stairs where
her own child's breath and breath kept coming.

Between midnight and five, the alarm set
for the blue feeding, cringed at its own sound,
its split entry into the cold brain.
She went down the stairs, the tiny mouth
pecking at her arm. Lit the candle left-handed
and sat. The flame churned in its wax,
making the wall kite with shapes
any eye could organize into trees, sky,
or in the corner, a spider walking its web.

Feeding,
the other breast weeping in sympathy.
Twenty degrees outside. Gold in the hoodlum grin
of the grate. She felt the thing hovering,
half-expected the candle to go,
like a bad fiilm. On the wall, the new shape
suddenly above her body, then settling.

She had come to hold them in her arms
and though she could no longer breathe
she made the sign of breath above them.
That was all, someone who'd held a child
to her heart in this room, returned.
When the baby slept,
she willed her visitor to stay,
mother-protector, then

willed her not to stay,
the light began to sway and her shadow
became mother-specter,

willed her not to stay as
those other things that lived in her,
such able-bodied failure
not even death could prevent it
from coming back,
the sun rose giddy on it,

and she must wake again
finding so many people to feed,
so much work to do.

After Care

You see the building falling down over there?
I come in to do my work when it's almost bare,
when the rats manage it

and if I may, I'll talk as I work,
washing the bodies of the dead squatters there,

under that sky the color
of a cigarette burn on a child's body.

In my line, I don't find
that too sensational a simile.
After care, after compassion

are outlasted by traffic
all night past the lit dock

of the morgue, after nobody
feels sorry for anybody anymore

it's there on the clockless wall
of the bar, the camera likewise
reducing death to the anecdotal:

the heap of small skulls down an airshaft
the kid dead at the starved mother's breast
forty days of blood spit in the torturer's dish
and what lies next to it . . .

what the righteous call the politics
of the matter, bent as they are on indenturing
the dead to their rhetoric.

Unlike them, I am most useful
afterwards
taking a shroud measurement
sponging the blood
pressing out the small fires
along the scalp

and I tell you when I shut
those fierce eyes and draw
the expression somewhere between
surprise and sexual gratitude

I feel I've done what no one else
has with love—I've made the dead,
for once, return it—

salvaged that last question
like a lock of hair thrown over
the shoulder, as each descends

the disappearing stairs.
I hold them up: eyes, lips, sexual wounds,
in what light we can still eke out of heaven
that bare swinging bulb under which

my hands work
for an effect we remember
long past compassion.

Nineteen Seventy

"A man in motion always devises an aim for that motion."
—War and Peace

Vladimir Lenin rocked back
and forth, then toppled
from his tall iron stilts,
nearly falling on me.

What a humiliating way to die
I remember thinking, *crushed
by a bad Social Realist sculpture.*

Instead the great man's bust
fell against the schoolroom window
and stared longingly out at the hills

of Minsk, where the statue of the boy-
martyr stood, flinging a home-
made grenade at a German tank.

He'd dislodged Lenin accidentally,
the young Intourist guide—
he'd been making eyes at me since
the border, at Brest. Now, having

invited me into the one-room schoolhouse,
away from the others, he'd turned suddenly
to me—to make, I suppose, some declaration,
and overturned the Father
of the Revolution, fitted up
in red centennial bunting.

He was shamed.
He bent over, grunting
as he wrestled the great geometric head
back up on its spindly props.

Outside, the green August shade deepened,
grew burnished as a brass samovar.
Early sunset. My fellow student
travelers, the British, stood

at the open rear doors of our van.
The guide dusted his hands, checked
his watch, his dickey soiled,
his Kennedy haircut drooping. We were

late, off the official itinerary,
in trouble. He tapped briskly
at the window to get their attention,
his smile in profile, strained, imploring—

like Rostov at the hunt, praying the wolf
come to him. *What*, he asked, *are they doing?*
It is eight hundred kilometers to Moscow.

I shrugged. *They have tea,* I said.
It is a national custom. We stood
at the window and stared—the Old Man's
eyes burned at our backs as we watched.

They were pouring from a flowered
china pot, passing Weetabix and cheese.
Minsk grew dark blue around their propane flame,
and above their heads, the brave young boy
lifted his metal fist to the sky,
to the locked face of invasion.

Monk's House, Rodmell

—for Lynne McMahon

In her bedroom,
she set a convex mirror on a stand,
so that when the visitor

looked in
expecting to see the familiar
line of lip and brow,

what appeared instead
was the head up-ended—
the mouth a talking wound

above
the eyes, upside down, fluttering,
like the eyes in the skull

of a calf slung on the blood-hook—
or a baby's lightning blink, dropped low
in the bone cage

about to be born

Walls washed down with the cold pardons of the nurse.
Gem green paint restored from old scrapings.
Here and there, a trifling, a lightening
beyond the author's original intent,
which was, in the drawing room, positively spleenish.
From razor bits of palette, touch-ups: Mrs. Woolf's favorite color.

The Trust ladies place the still-ticking brain
of Leonard's wireless next to the empty brass stalk
with its single blossom: old black hat
she wore like pharaoh gazing down
the Nile-green Nile.

That's her:
that flat drainboard of a face
set so fiercely against the previous
owner's trompe l'oeil beard and jug.

The simpleton's request: a picture of her young—
So the trees walk up burning,
the birds speak Latin
for the dull witted, drenched palette

the glimpse of whirlwind in the pond
where their handfuls of ash
drifted down

        and over
the great mown meadow next door
where the Rodmell August Fair is on.
My daughter astride a steam engine,
bored as any child
with the past. Later makes an X
(her favorite letter) with two sticks

held up to the window
of the great writer's garden study.

But the mirror standing in the air
a glass knot tying and retying itself

would repolarize, and she, drawing near,
reverse herself. A woman's rapt beautiful face
drawn downward by gravity, sorrow,
lit upward by the flame of age—
could turn over, floating, then submerge, amniotic!

Across the green from her bedroom window
she saw it: a fin cleaving dark waters—
"and that became *The Waves*." The ladies sip and look.

            Vanessa, pregnant,
laughing, crosses the garden. Two women
walk among the hollyhocks with shears.
The hedge dented by one's fluttering hands.
Inside her sister's body: fluttering hands.

            Annie's white sweater catches
on the thorns of blackberry canes. I pull her free
then pick six little ones, busy, like the swarm cells
of a fetus. Or the enlarging failure in those rooms,
unchecked growth: death-drawn, claustrophobic.

The wind, up from the South Downs,
blew the two women across the garden,
their shadows like crossed sticks. Sisters.
One shrugging slightly, a loose mauve shawl.
Where her sculpted head sits now, a stone wall.

She sat at this table
eating mutton and bread.
He was talking about the socialist initiative
and she turned away: someone was knocking
at the window. It was the French photographer
we surprised on our way out,
shooting the forbidden
interior through the dark glass.

Pick-Up Sticks

Twenty days between pictures,
beard grown in, back turned,
her husband builds things in the garage.
The electric saw shrieks
through the split wood.
The scream cuts off
the familiar voices
inside the house, the dull
buzz of scenes: kitchen
to living room to bedroom—
where the bed is neatly made
though the child's pick-up sticks
stay scattered on the rug.

Then a voice on the phone
hopes they can negotiate.
Hopes he will take
a flight to some city
where he will become
somebody fantastically competent—
say the pilot of a spacecraft,
or maybe someone sympathetic,
the average joe in denim jacket,
you know, the typical guy
left alone to raise four kids?

Wardrobe will call.
And she will replay
the saw bearing down
on the awl-worked juncture,
the instant, bedside, when the phone
rings and the wood falls free
of the serrate blade. In the wake:
shocked dust, her jagged call
carrying through the walls
of all that is unactable.

Immunity

Issa's little daughter, Sato-jo,
on all fours in this haiku, laughs!
She's nearly my daughter's age
when he makes her immortal.

Her face contains his,
like a reflection of sun
that leaps from wave to wave—
still, if real age is in the expression,

she's sure enough of love
to have begun moving away.
One step, two. How the body
sways away from its origins,

the parents, the mourners
who laugh and clap.
I look up into sunlight, Annie
in her flowered suit pressing

her hands on the moon rocket
printed on the bottom of the pool.
Two haiku, two seasons blown gently
apart by her breath: Sato-jo

dying of smallpox, Issa bending
over her, light surrounding them
like a moat. The burning wire
between them, silence: the same

soundless echo Hokusai paints
between the great wave, poised,
and the doomed fishing boats below.
And these, haiku: two opposed

notions of perfection:
The fat baby serene, New Year's Day.
Then autumn winds scattering
the red blossoms she loved to pluck.

Either her death or her life.
Neither will he liken to anything.
Not her soul to a kite.
Not the kite to a marker,

bearing the name of a child
running on the earth below it.
Nothing but water pouring into water.
Spring ending. Him holding her

in that moment of immunity,
before the dream
rises in its tree
of new bloomed resistance
into this future

where I wrap her in a towel,
I carry her in my arms.
I take her death into me
little by little—temple bells, grass—

happiness
when she smiles like this
when I see she'll live forever.

Meal Ticket

Qhyoum could be a caddy, or a cook—
that summer in Kashmir he drove cab
for the two Americans. Doubled as guide,
shopping front, fisherman: he drove them
to the Wangat River high in the Himalayas
and waded white water by *her* side,
he sunburned and begged off. They fried trout
with the *shikari*, she noticed him eating
ravenously, hair in his eyes. So young,
he was to make his *haj* soon with a bride
he'd not yet met. Soon, when he finished school.
When it flooded, he kept them away from
his family's sunken houseboat in the Jhelum—
was it shame? Her hand next to his on the English
grammar pulled from the glove compartment,
explaining the subjunctive's *wish* or *would*.
Hot weather at the airport the night they left.
At the door, he'd pulled away from them
in sudden distaste, to join a crowd of Moslem
youths. She called to him when the plane was late—
she'd passed up the dull consolation meal,
thought of him: *take this* she called, but he turned away,
his stern friends scowling at her Stones T shirt.
She shrugged and let the ticket flutter.
Later, boarding arm in arm with *him*, she'd heard
her name called louder and more frantically—
he was pushing alone through the crowd—
the *ticket* he cried, his eyes bulged—
when she told him, puzzled, he fixed her with
that look: furious pity or passionate disbelief,
which, as she entered the plane and looked back,
appeared nothing more than purest hunger.

August 1974: A Tapestry

Threading terror into the beautiful rugs,
the skeletal little boys of Kashmir
lifted fingers so sure of the whip

they wove the whip deep into the warp—
into the heart of the emperor's city
the branches of bruised fruit,
the red beaks of the talking birds.

A flinch lifted the mouth of the courtesan
into a trifle foxier sneer,
a lash stroke electrified the tassels

on the floating pillows beneath
the cross-legged soothsayers,
green jewels exploded from
a queen's amulet

like new seeds from a dried pod.
Backward glances in the tapestry!
Fear, lyrical in flaws,
and still within tradition:

in this country oppression
often married beauty to aberration.
In the marketplace near the houseboats
she'd seen the requisite one-eyed parrot
and two-headed snake. Collared hawks
and insect shapes of opium.
Here the rugs were cheaper.

Weave her now, the young American woman.
Lately a tourist, this morning a traveling Marxist
exhorting the foreman to throw off
his bosses. *Weave in* how he bows, speaks
English a little, shows her his gums

then snaps the lash over the head
of an eight-year-old who stares
and loses the beat. *Weave* the chanter
calling out the pattern, the photos
of stolen Tibetan rugs tacked like pin ups

to the frame of the loom. In one,
three blurs in fur earflaps
hold up a secret pattern:
a panel of flowers and serpents
uncoiling from the head of the Buddha sleeper.

Weave the story inside the rug
pawned by tired thieves
within the dark margins of the Himalayas

within the photograph in the hot dusty
room where the sun frames them:
the angry young woman, the foreman nodding

meekly, brandishing the whip,
split suddenly into myriad multicolored
threads as the shuttle is thrown
and the chanter chants the pattern

(she says she will write about this,
                    she will return)
and light pauses lovingly on the curved
gleam of the razor in the powerful fist
                    of the imperturbable cutter.

Asbestos

It belongs to us and to this world,
though it enters through force,
though forced, refuses to burn
or be divisible past the bright eyelash

of fiber, refined, it is. Charlemagne
ordered a tablecloth made of it
and dined thereon in a kind of extended
punchline: a maid threw it in the fire

to clean, yanked it out again, gleaming, intact!
The guests, expected to witness
and exclaim as guests so often
are made to do at dinner parties, did,

thinking perhaps more highly of the roast fowl
than their host. Or the sugar castle
borne in on a tray, its turrets tweaked-looking.
Up in the Urals everyday, tons are freed

from the rock. Then the jaws of the crushing
machines yawn and the snow falls over it
with its silent clang, and clang, the railroad cars
hitch up to bear it East and West

into the windless stalls where rocket shields
and launch pad walls are built by robots.
In the meantime, the little servant girl
throws the cloth in the flames and pulls it

out again; the guests applaud.
The robot hand moves the blazing wall,
the stanchions ripple in the heat,
and something changes shape invisibly

as when our fathers, back from the War,
unrolled it like bandages. Yards of it,
pressed into service, wrapped tight to insulate
                    the house and kids.

The white python twisted round a pipe,
slept a forty-year sleep,
breathing its colorless dust into our lungs.

                Tell the carcinogenic emperor
what went wrong has little to do with evil intent.
Originally, we expected to kill no one—
then, somehow, everyone in the world.

                We had these glorious and useless
personalities and we had to applaud ourselves
so that we could recompose, time and again,
against nature's own odds. Like a dear mutant, self-made,

                    like the woman's name painted
on the bomber, gleaming as it groans over the target city,
which boils up below: houses and trees and little people!

and we're pulled clean each time from the fire,
each time young, each time brave, each time free.

Applause*

—for Paul Monette

1

Not the glittering shudder in the ear, the high whine of the wasp,
Not the drunk holding up a glass, getting eloquent; nor
percussive, furious, the steady drum on the desk of the child

who doesn't get it. Not the echoing blow to the right temple
of the guard patrolling the green lawns of the industrial giant,
the hail of stones and beer cans onstage at the rock concert—

nor the thunk-thunk of a pistol whipping,
the eerie scree of someone screwing gun to silencer.
Applause has no opposite, contains its own poles—
yet it might be said the the soundlessness of the newly dead,

the preternaturally silent chorus of, in this news photograph,
a family, drowned on their way here from Haiti is audible.
still afloat, lashed to their tiny illegal raft—hands folded
together, like this, like applause for the end, the soul's tortured bow
                                                              and exit.

*Title of a photographic exhibit by Holly Wright.

40

2

Applause has a place: punctual comment,
forever hearing itself, even in a mob. As if clapping
is thought, a glass hatch high above everything, but
occasionally caught off-guard—like the woman or man
who moves air traffic across the skies, psyching out
the 3-D screen, piping the scoop in the earphones direct
to the pilots. Those steady voice blips, split suddenly with deific
                                              chitter,

surprise! God is a space chimp, communicating
from his little phobic cell circling earth, razzing the planets.
Intercepting the perfunctory handoff, airport to port,
the altitude drift—God the screecher, God the stomper,
God the whistler in the balcony: they listen to plain static,
hungry for his holy voice, his Bronx cheers. God in his tiny
monkey spacesuit, chewing up the tubes of all the technology
he never mastered, God the Glitch, clapping his ugly furry little
                                                 mitts.

3

You're clapping. In the photo for Holly's exhibit,
One shot of each subject, face and hands, maybe thirty in all,
each photo on the wall of a circular room and the people
photographed are applauding. If you stand in the center
of that room, they applaud *you*.

        Nice conceit. Nice comment
on perspective. Nice immediate drift toward the philosophical.
Like Goya, the pure strain on the image can bend to political
                argument.

See that fat man clapping? He's mean, he doesn't want to do it,
but others are, so he tries to make his rhythm revisionist, one half
                second off.
See the other guy, preoccupied, going over his bills in his head
as he claps? Or the woman in the flowered hat, thrilled
to be an audience, thrilled to be a pair of long, black theater gloves,
             one thrilled glass eye?

4

Straight into the eyes of you, a real close-up,
making those palms applauding an unnatural act—
but so what? you seem to say. Your gaze labors to be direct:
too aware of the ironies of the so-called candid shot.
You look like a theatergoer, lit by the shifting prism
of stagelight. Ladies, gentlemen, the audience takes
its seat in familiar anonymity, but wait—
your hands keep meeting in midair.
You don't stop clapping, even after the others do.
That's who she photographed, seventh row, no heckler,
but you in that instant you don't stop, you go on
applauding every moment, though I know that's my projection.
Because your friend is in the photograph next to you—
still alive then, so joyous, I don't think I've ever seen a man look
that happy.

5

I suppose it happened something like this.
A woman got up (because the moon was full, because
her newborn was going to live now, after all, because
the fire of dung and grass did not, for once, go out)—
and began to dance. She moved her hips inside the animal skin,
the firelight made her look so huge that he loved her
and wanted just to see her there attached to her great shadow.
Seeing her shuffle and hop, he started to make a sound
with his hands. She looked up. It was not the slap of bare feet
on stone, not the bones of the dead in the wind, but a bearded
ugly appreciator she would come to call by name. He was saying
with his hands: I am looking at you and you are my delight
and this sound makes clear who I am. I am the one watching
you and saying it is good, making my two hands the collision of
love and power.

6

Grape laboring over grape out of dark green leafage,
out of the woven balsa strips of the scuppernong, set
against the white stucco wall of the garage, set off-kilter
like a leaf crown sliding over the eye of Bacchus. Years later,
in Perugia, in the blue valley at wine harvest, I found
the sweet life-source of it, that image, the bare-bottomed
children in the mother's arms, the vat of grape, the handclap
at dusk in the cobbled street: *come home.* The day of his funeral,
your friend, I noticed the arbor near the Chapel of Memory,
rife with pale blue-green grapes against the white tiles. I
didn't think of wine, or new-minted money—I thought of
a shift downward from thought as they brought the coffin past,
a cliché of hearing: waves, cicadas, or the wind's slow applause
through the graveyard trees—it was just that sound seemed so
necessary—a dog barking, a plane—something of this life to
                                        salute him, anything.

7

Well, what did we expect? You and I
were joking once that the self is a path
of stepping-stones sinking in the black water:
now the self is nothing more than a sound.
Like the dawn rain, *om*, anahat, 4th Chakra,
the sound of two things *not* hitting
together. Annie draws faces in the air with her finger,
expects us to see who and where they are, say
excuse me when we walk through them. *Excuse me,*
I'm walking through my ex-lovers, my mother and father,
I'm walking through Jesus and Coco Chanel, Torquemada
and Simone Weil, poets living and dead, *excuse me*—
sound waves of one person standing up,
clapping the whole time, not for an encore, but for the end,
$$\text{the end of it.}$$

8

In irresistible eclipse, two shadow jets converge
on the cypher green screen: the controller spills
his coffee, screaming into the mouthpiece of the headset.
Gets drifting static, the wind, night, fog. He
doesn't see the sky light up once, twice, two hundred
miles south, but he sways in place and calls them to him:
pilot, flight attendants, the woman in the fifteenth row
nursing her infant, the toddler racing up and down the aisles
(stopped forever midstride), the elderly vacationers,
the whole living matrix, sitting tight in a horseshoe,
flung out there beyond direction. Huddled like an audience,
or the gallery of people pictured applauding, while
the dark figure in the spotlight beckons—they stay so animated,
so still, refusing to imagine it: the act of relinquishing thought,
then joining whatever it is in that huge specific light onstage.

9

Walked in to polite applause. (The teacher-keepers
had insisted: *be nice or else*.) Thirty-six or so
teenage mothers, runaways, JD's, misfits, abused
babies. They looked, at first, like one big leer:
Impress us, poet-ess. God, should I read Plath?
Then it came back to me: the raw gleam of those nights
at Rikers. Poems of the oil spill, the ruptured tanker
roiling on the top-water, sullen ink on the inmates' fingers,
then a torch hits the slick: flames
skyscraper-high. These brows furrow the same,
they write their Letters to God, Mamma, or an Unborn
Child. Here's a hurt girl, head down, reading hers—
from a dead kid. "Don't do what my mamma did
to me, with drugs: —*I was like a butterfly wrapped
in a cocoon. She cut my wings, then my eyes, she ripped
my five senses, she wove that white powder into my shroud*.

10

It was After Care, the name of the program,
some obscure branch of New York City services.
Our job: to find jobs for "ex-offenders," newly ex.
A simple task? For a twenty-four-year-old
student of Marcuse, enemy of the state? Piece of cake.
Fast talk. I called up Chase Manhattan—
You mean you *don't* want to hire a first-class
booster to work in the vault? Or Ma Bell:
Good with numbers I said of the hooker in front
of me. Ma said no, so did the hooker. Why should
she scrape for ninety bucks a week when a good night
brought six hundred? *Dumb flatback!* She sneered,
clapped when a friend said she wanted to go straight.
"You sittin' on your money-maker!" I heard that quote over
and over that hot summer, on the phone, sweating.
I sat flat on my money-maker, using my big money-loser
to rethink economic politics. But then, I've always been
surprised to find the world just the way the cynics made it.

11

What happens to that youthful formality of purpose?
(I feel like I'm lost, do you? Listening to everyone
applauding a play I missed.) Spring here in L.A. today,
ninety or so, everything in bloom. I drive my four-
year-old to preschool and turn off Santa Monica
into a stakeout. Top-lit cop cars jacknifed onto lawns,
a chopper churning the smog, an amplified voice:
Give up while you can. Come out with your hands raised.
My kid doesn't look up from her book, *The Big Orange Splot.*
All the hyper-tense police phrasing doesn't phase her.
I stare at a woman on the curb, solemnly applauding
the police—as if this is a film set. Perhaps it is.
But who's in that house? Finally, we're allowed to pass,
the choppers hang and sway. *Who was in that house?*
I woke, wondering, today, and who's in my life in this aftershock
of shock, L.A.?

12

Each day's lack of point is why we lower ourselves
between armrests in the false dark to see what some
overpaid auteur lusts after. We go on because of the
lack of distance applause lends to distance—we clap
not so much to judge as to be that other character,
the one offstage who knows the most—therefore most hurt,
pleased, or estranged. Applauding applause. One day a while
before he died, you came over with him. Annie was napping
in her crib and he touched her head and said
sleep well honey. I wanted to cheer him for going on
like that, for blessing my child when he knew he was dying—
and when the raft hit the swells, one after the other;
they held on and prayed and God laughed, God gave them a hand.
That was what God liked most, circling in his capsule,
when they beamed the messages out on the great radio
                                                telescopes—
We're here, here's a picture of us, third from the sun,
here's DNA, a human baby—and a V for peace!
He sent them his holy static, from all the way back
to the Bang, when he first thought of it, the sound of clapping,
on the seventh day, as he sat back, as he rested.

About the Author

Carol Muske was born in St. Paul, Minnesota, in 1945. She received her M.A. in 1970 from the State University of California at San Francisco, and she has taught in the graduate writing programs at Columbia University, the Iowa Writers' Workshops, the University of California at Irvine, and the University of Virginia. Her first book of poems, *Camouflage*, was published in 1975 in the Pitt Poetry Series. It was followed by *Skylight* (1981) and *Wyndmere* (1985). Among her awards are the 1979 Alice Fay Di Castagnola Award of the Poetry Society of America, a 1981 John Simon Guggenheim Fellowship, and a 1984 National Endowment for the Arts Poetry Fellowship. Muske presently teaches at the University of Southern California. She lives in Los Angeles with her husband, actor David Dukes, her stepson Shawn, and her daughter Annie Cameron.

PITT POETRY SERIES

Ed Ochester, General Editor